The Magic Pot

Rajesh Lavlekar

JYOTSNA PRAKASHAN

The Magic Pot : JP 155

Published by : Milind L. Paranjape
Jyotsna Prakashan, 'Dhavalgiri'
430-31 Shaniwar Peth, Pune 411030

Mumbai Office : Mohan Building,
162 J. Shankarshet Marg, Girgaum, Mumbai 400004

First Edition : 2011 Reprint : 2016

Printed by : Unique Offset, Narhegaon, Pune 411041

Price : Rs 75/-

ISBN 978-81-7925-279-6

1. The Magic Pot

Once there were four friends - crow, sparrow, monkey and cat.

One day they decided to have a feast of *khir-puri.*

The monkey brought wood from the forest. The cat brought milk.

The crow got the utensils. The sparrow brought rice, sugar, and sooji.

The monkey prepared the fireplace.

The cat mixed the sugar, sooji, milk and began to stir the *khir* on the fire.

When it was cooked, the friends danced in joy.

The monkey then kneaded the dough. The sparrow made small balls from it.

While the crow
heated oil in a frying pan,
the cat rolled out
the *puris*.

The monkey
fried them.

He suggested, "Let's go to the river for a dip." The crow and sparrow readily agreed.

The cat declined. "I can't bear cold water. I'll stay behind and guard the place. You can go," she said. The three friends went and enjoyed themselves in the river.

Here, the cat found the *khir-puri* very tempting.

She ate up everything. Then quietly sat near the fireplace.

The trio returned from the river feeling extremely hungry.

"My stomach is paining," said the cat. "You go ahead and eat. I'm not hungry."

They got ready
to have their meal.

The monkey opened
the *puri* container,
and was shocked to
find it empty!

He uncovered
the *khir* vessel.
It too was empty!
All the three asked
the cat. "Who ate
the *khir-puri* ?"
The cat kept quiet.

A heated argument followed. Just then a rabbit arrived. It was decided that he should solve the mystery.

The rabbit picked a water-pot, and took everyone to the river. Turning it upside down, he said, "Each one of you must sit on this magic pot. No sooner the culprit sits, it will sink."

The sparrow sat first. She chirped, “Am I guilty, am I not, Sink and tell oh magic pot.”
The pot did not sink.

The crow sat next. He cawed, “Am I guilty, am I not, Sink and tell oh magic pot.”
The pot did not sink.

Then the monkey sat. He hooped, “Am I guilty, am I not, Sink and tell oh magic pot.”
The pot did not sink.

Finally it was the cat's turn. 'Since I've eaten the *khir-puri,* the pot is sure to sink,' she thought.

She panicked, and ran away speedily. "Thief, thief," the others shouted, and ran after her.

2. The Greedy Wolf

A greedy wolf once chanced upon a dead deer. While gobbling it up hungrily, a small bone got stuck in his throat.

His friend, the fox, rang a bell and proclaimed on his behalf: "Whoever removes the bone from the wolf's throat will be richly rewarded."

The rabbit gloated, "Good punishment for the wicked wolf!"

"Let him die in agony," said the peacock.

The antler remarked,
"Although I can remove
the bone with my horn,
I will not help
that cunning wolf."

Finally a crane removed the bone with his long beak.

He immediately demanded his reward.

The wolf retorted, "The fact that your neck has come out intact from my mouth is in itself a reward. So go away!"

3. The Cunning Monkey

Once two cats found a large chunk of butter, and began fighting over it.

A monkey watched them from a distance.

Going near he said,
"Stop fighting. I'll divide
the butter equally for you."

He brought a weighing
scale and began to make
two halves of the butter.

The pan in which
he put more butter
went down.

He scooped some
butter from it
and gulped it.

He weighed
the butter again.

Since he had eaten
from one pan,
the other pan
became heavier.

Quickly he ate
a bit from it.

In this way the entire butter
disappeared.

Throwing aside the
weighing scale, the
monkey ran away,
leaving the cats
dazed and gaping!

4. The Monkey and The Crocodile

A monkey once lived next to a jamun tree by the riverside.
Extremely fond of jamuns, whenever they ripened, one would always see him on the tree.

One day a crocodile saw him drinking water. She felt tempted to eat him.

Coming close to the bank she began chatting with him.

"There's a guava tree across the river," she said. "Want to come? I'll carry you on my back."

The thought of guavas made the monkey's mouth water. Innocently, he readily agreed.

Taking him on her back, the crocodile began to swim.

Half way across
she exclaimed,
"You foolish monkey!
I want your heart.
I'm going to kill you
by drowning."

With great presence of mind
the monkey replied,
"My heart is on the jamun tree.
If you take me back,
I'll give it to you."

He then began to
flatter the crocodile.
"You look beautiful,
and your back is so
soft. Take me back
quickly. Don't you want
my heart?"

Immensely pleased
by this flattery,
the crocodile took
the monkey back.

No sooner did they
reach the river-bank,
the monkey jumped
on the tree.

Gleefully he
chuckled, "Lady,
my heart is not here!
When it's found,
I'll send it to you.
Goodbye!"

5. The Mouse and The King

There once lived a mouse who loved to roam around.

One day he found a piece of cloth.

He took it to the *dhobi*
to get it washed.

"Wash this cloth for me,"
he said to the *dhobi*.

"I will not wash your cloth,"
the *dhobi* replied.
"Don't disturb me."

"I'll go to the king
and bring the police,"
threatened the mouse.
"Then I'll watch the fun."

The *dhobi* got frightened.
"No, no," he begged.
"Don't bring the police.
I'll wash your cloth."

He washed
the cloth clean.

The mouse took the
cloth in grand style
to the tailor.

“Stitch a beautiful cap for me,” he said to the tailor.

“I will not stitch a cap for you,” shouted the tailor angrily. “Don’t pester me.”

“I’ll go to the king and bring the police,” Threatened the mouse. “Then I’ll watch the fun.”

The tailor got frightened.
"No, no," he pleaded.
"Don't bring the police.
I'll stitch a cap for you."

He stitched a cap
for the mouse.

The mouse came home
and admired himself
in front of the mirror.

"It will look better with a tassel," he thought.

He went to the tassel-maker and said, "Put a lovely red tassel on this."

"I've got no time today," replied the tassel-maker. "I won't do it."

"I'll go to the king and bring the police," threatened the mouse. "Then I'll watch the fun."

The tassel-maker got frightened. He quickly put a tassel on the cap.

With his cap perched jauntily, the mouse went to meet the king.

The king was riding down
the road on his horse.

The mouse
climbed up a tree
to get a closer view.

The king came
right under the tree,
and as the mouse was
about to call out....

His cap fell down
in front of the king.

"To whom does this
beautiful cap belong?"
the king enquired.

"It is mine," said the
mouse. "Give it back."

"No, I will not!"
the king retorted.
"I have liked it."

Immediately the mouse rushed home and fetched his *dholak.* "Dum dum dida, dum dum dida," he cried. "The king is a beggar, he's taken my cap, The king is a beggar, he's taken my cap."

Ashamed at being called a beggar, the king promptly returned the cap.

The mouse beat on his *dholak* and cried joyfully,
"The king is a coward,
he's returned my cap,
The king is a coward..."